DISSONANCE

PHOENIX POETS

Edited by Srikanth Reddy

Rosa Alcalá, Douglas Kearney &
Katie Peterson, consulting editors

Dissonance

KRISTIN DYKSTRA

THE UNIVERSITY OF CHICAGO PRESS
CHICAGO & LONDON

The University of Chicago Press, Chicago 60637
The University of Chicago Press, Ltd., London
©2025 by The University of Chicago
Published 2025
Printed in the United States of America

34 33 32 31 30 29 28 27 26 25   1 2 3 4 5

ISBN-13: 978-0-226-84031-4 (paper)
ISBN-13: 978-0-226-84032-1 (e-book)
DOI: https://doi.org/10.7208/chicago/9780226840321.001.0001

Library of Congress Cataloging-in-Publication Data

Names: Dykstra, Kristin, author.
Title: Dissonance / Kristin Dykstra.
Description: Chicago : The University of Chicago Press, 2025. | Series: Phoenix poets
Identifiers: LCCN 2024035539 | ISBN 9780226840314 (paperback) | ISBN 9780226840321 (ebook)
Subjects: LCGFT: Prose poems. | Photographs.
Classification: LCC PS3604.Y498 D47 2025 | DDC 811/.6—dc23/eng/20240820
LC record available at https://lccn.loc.gov/2024035539

♾ This paper meets the requirements of ANSI/NISO Z39.48-1992 (Permanence of Paper).

J'ai pris sans éclat le poignet de l'équinoxe

RENÉ CHAR, Calendrier

I have quietly taken the wrist of the equinox

RENÉ CHAR, Calendar,
trans. Nancy Kline

CONTENTS

Examine the structure for its prototype, and under the ridgelines, you find a road.

Roads, generally speaking, lead to other prototypes. Here, foothills. A place in minds, in laws, in maps, in practice, in dissonance.

> Origin: Formed within English, by compounding. Originally *U.S.* Any of a group of hills next to a mountain or mountain range. Chiefly in *plural*.

People head into the hills when goaded by need. Which one? To be parted from self. To start down a new road. To shelter at a remove. To flare into gesture. To burn need out of self. Some move with a foreboding of cataclysm, hoping to turn days toward an alternate sun, and their actions rotate gesture, and figure, and general contour of road.

History flares too, and then compounding actions will be taken for the people, without consent. Blurring their figures, me you us they.

To move through foothills: witness transitionals. Foothills are neither the low nor the high point of a landscape. A view from within foothills is not a wide-angle vista—you see those from seats of power on the high ridges or along land so flat that it evokes the curvature of the earth. Within hills, you grasp land and sky in segments.

> View from the F-35 fighter jet—?

On the ground: dirt roads must be remade—laboriously, continuously—
on any day in all seasons, after weather has worn their structures too hard.

People in hills, plural.

DISSONANCE

FIRST

It's daybreak. Who are you? Setting a foot

       outward, toward a ridge;

       inward, toward a firmament.

Foothills all around: an intermediary place, five degrees cooler than the lowlands. Disengage/reengage.

When I cast my self out of my self, see, it's a separation of two forms.

Mail car creeps along a dirt road, course charted. Figure inside measures the road into mailboxes, into the cost of mileage piling on the car, mileage along with the mud, the car that does not belong to the state, car lost incrementally to roads, future running down with each delivery, stretching dinner into one next day, breakfast from one day into the next, lunch from day into day, the figure pulls the car to one side.

Children run back and forth across a collapsing wall, breaking the rules.

The fullness of the wind masks disturbances comprising the landscape.

Or is that fog, melding all things that fail to connect. Lines silver with sap.

What forms brush each other?

Once upon a time I was that. Then I became not that.

Statements—

In the valley, one figure sinks in among others. But elsewhere someone is on the move. Dirt road bends upward house toward house, away from a village toward a village, no turning away, valley toward hill toward mountain, yellow, heat rising into cool, no turning away, toward rain, these turns stringing law up and down, within 100 miles of an external boundary—

Hush: Have you seen the place as a whole or stripped of all its symbolism?

How animals look from an F-35 fighter jet.

Where one north lies. After the Great Depression, people left cities again in search of land; some went north. Figures who disappeared into the hills: transplants. Few places inside the hills look down upon lake, or look out at anything other than a ridge, a short length of road, and the green. The richness of the earth, its minerals: some hardscrabble hills, some richer in calcium to the west, a slow fabrication of happiness. One, looking down: *Over the lake a white wall was advancing, driving foam before it. The mountains sank down in the white, the wind began to sing.* Vibration. *The rain is rain, and for me and my lips and body.* Those who lost someone in the hills. Those who will.

Is there an us? Walking with an unnerved dog, one figure steps through familiar woods. Back in winter another glided slowly on skis, followed by a dog in narrow tracks. One heartbeat follows another. If the dog doesn't get in the way, this is order. What if the dog gets in the way? Gilded, summer will be the dog's time, a time of no longer inhaling bleach from floors inside the remembered shelter, a time when a dog is not abandoned by a person but abandoned to its own paths and investigations. Rich odors layered in mud. Those curtailed routes whose logic circles incessantly back, a being, present inside its own presence. The edge defining one desire interrupts the forward motion of another.

The children wonder aloud what friends are doing.

Channels wash out loaded branches crack. One road as a whole now.
One road it is not now.

Enclosed commuters thump past what strange thing will she be doing in ten
more years. Rapid repeat, all this from the car, from the next car, from the car
still to come. Dirt to be sprayed sideways by the car.

Mutterings from the dead. The horizon moved. Or it didn't.

Planning board debates sidewalk development down in the growing town.
Where lines *fail to connect*. Now offering creemees too.

Out there? Less green. Rumors of an interior checkpoint.

Some numerous presence, *who grows blunt through premonitions.*

Anticipate, before the landscape changes.

On the western end of the road: Hinesburg. First library built in 1810 to hold lowland memories. Current library, a hardware store converted after 1996 to house tilting visions of who the figures were, who they are, what forms their minds will take.

[What is it that seems so, and yet is not? Sightings from the bookshelves: Boxes monster wizard play table corner screen cartoon Athena. The all-Vermont shelf, signs and voices inside these walls, 1934 *From This Hill Look Down* chapters, transplanted drought the rain barter, signs and voices inside these walls, storage winter harvest portraits, contrarian bilingual dreams, bluegrass holiday songfest spotting stars, signs and voices inside, Orion time passes headphones about the seasons, they seem so, this seems so, we are told we seem.]

[Inside these walls, kid detective new releases banned books, regulars in corners, voices, graphic novel naturalists sparring with scientists who sneer at naturalists strata epochs, signs and, coral under trees why rain falls onto the ground energy efficiency, signs and voices inside these, reintroduction of the American marten *Northern Woodlands*, now, these walls, *Vermont Public Documents Being Reports of State Officers, Departments, and Institutions, For the Two Years Ending June 30, 1918* auditors patrolmen intoxicating liquor counties, care of the insane, ritual attacks, signs and voices, missing "h" in -burg names stripped of British flourish after 1890, shark teeth, signs inside these walls, the order, stones removed to till soil, stones relocated into walls. The weight we gave every such thing.]

[Signs and voices inside these walls, large-print books, front center new mystery new biography new fiction new young adult, voices inside these walls, how-to orientation to the stars, season with kosher salt and fresh-ground pepper, two white gourds and a holiday ghost, signs and voices, disorder. Sightings: one crow, a chain of crows, if disorder issued forth from the building, if this spring the crows made their way, signs, to the intersection, across before the high school, stepping through the eastward wind toward green mountains, voices, hopping straight when the road shifts north, hold eastward, up into the road, through hills, onward. That which grows weighty with life, that which does not: held within, or loosed throughout the mind?]

Chainsaws running in late spring. That pile is bigger than this pile. Figure stacking one neat pile now, one neat pile later, seeing piles to come, piles that should come but won't. The afternoon light, refracting: time equals hours of heat in the winter, segments further divided by species of wood, some burn long, some burn fast. You are silver and gold, who's got some kindling left. Will weave an airy pile while this hemisphere leans toward the sun. Drop twigs and birchbark in a tub. Split more wood. What is the future value, or whether night could be enough. Night, refuser of accumulation; fire, unsayer of accumulation. What you see: necessities, those blanks where the piles are not.

The children hum nearby.

Where the north lies. Northern New England lies mostly within 100 miles of an external border. Do you live inside a hundred-mile zone maybe so most of us do. *Numerous presence Bienvenue*, reside within laws strewn across your hundred miles. Poke holes through their layers, head for the hills. Witness the frantic creation of vulnerabilities. Figures fabricate vague threats above borderscapes, aching for the Cold War world quest for the best *bipolar clash*. Rituals of gathering clouds. Or, their concrete, funded outcomes. How many newly hired agents? A ballooning glare out of sight yet nearby, the grail called forth from billows of fantasy. Now hiring. *The center operates 24 hours a day, seven days a week, 365 days a year.* Now hiring. To grasp at some people. Hands gesture. Underdocumented official hands, rapidly withdrawn from sight. Checkpoints appear and disappear, concretely cloudy. The smell of caged children travels. Leaves here go on filtering sky and indignities. Everywhere the agents multiplied across our time. What dreams endure a childhood?

Those present who live secret unto even themselves. Pain, a contour for all days. Haze sits lightly in the eyes, dust rises over the cadaver at the side of the road, a grimy garter snake. Curves that will never meet— People of the world advocate for beavers: who build deserts back to green, recentering the weight of the mind.

A package truck barrels down the road. Someone inside calculates the road by package drops. Another course charted. No: two lives that bifurcate. With any drop a spurt of time, gushes of road driven versus time running with feet on the ground, training time, life of waking to the road, which will always happen later, never in this drop-time, on this new-summer heat-road holding off the real time, only a fragment of now, the now is after the final drop, sorted.

The beaver house is there, but no figure for beaver. The beaver dam is there, but no figure for beaver. A gap, where branches still hold green leaves, figures beaver. More green leaves grow. If they multiply, a beaverpond shifts into beavermeadow. Northern watersheds measure their futures in transition: a year abandoned, some years still vacant, then reoccupied with beaverfigures. Water lines a newly defined edge against the empty air. But the flood came: beaver disappeared. The pond margin holds. Are there aspens, or cottonwoods, or oaks or ashes, any pole-sized ones, a winter food supply? Two-year-old beavers searching for new ponds get hit on roads every spring. Where is the beaver now, where did we go?

The national strategic community listens. So the military author of the Vermont wind-power report asserts. In certain directions only, ears turned away from other lines. Connecting as things connect. Author asserts: an effort to tip the group mind. Out of unsustainable force and into a new strategic ecosystem. Asserts: next, find a ridgeline for a power station. The community listens. Learn the sounds of interdependent power. The swish of law, not its bang. Or was that a strand of saffron. Finger your tangles of need and desire under every ridge. To be nothing, to be as the moment, to evaporate. Pale sparks across a power cell. One election cycle down the road, someone else's assertion: put a stop to thoughts.

SECOND

Isolated figure trots down a dirt road, at the start of day, not the same day as the other days, not the same day to be seen by people to come. Dust flaps pointers at sky. This one trots the day along one lane, passed by one oncoming car. The face of [X], one possible future. Or did they proliferate madly. If the road were an infinite surface, it wouldn't get so easily carved. Rainwater wouldn't cut the channels, road crews wouldn't fill them.

Figure at a screen working far off, which is right here, which is far from far, which is near. Pain is being today. The contract will expire soon, the far-off will rotate toward a different horizon. Like great telescopes roll toward worlds unseen. Toward many more faces and their blazings of interaction. An aureola glimmers, flickering its window shades at the night. Pain travels. Is disconnection possible now. Just one person huddled over one screen, one who will vanish down the road, later. The saffron thought floats on.

The children refuse food.

Builder of one's own home pounds another shingle with independence, plans the next shingle with independence, gets interrupted and might come back another day to finish the job. The independence lives inside that space between the faces, but back to the job at hand: When the builder looks away, the house wobbles. When the builder looks away, a memory. Gifts left behind by the dead. These were the visions . . . On the next hill is a little free library box nailed to a fat pole by the road. Also independent, in a neat schoolhouse shape. Not a box holding your past but still a box for your memory. *I made it myself.*

The children pull out stones holding a wall in place.

Forms gabbling down the summer road: sled dogs dragging ATVs. Riders thinking of snows, of time earning money and time not, of weather earning money and weather not, snows falling, snows failing. Tourists riding dogsleds. Where one lifetime is contained. Between changes to microclimates: the last winter was pocked with rains. Wheels knock on stones. Night: dogs bay at shadows from bear, bobcat, fisher. How long will their collars endure how long the bones. The owl flutes. Again it flutes: all that settling into spaces between.

The children appear, holding a colander with tomatoes, parsley, some too-small carrots.

Litterfall from white pines that comes too early, after warmer and wetter springs. Figures tread speculations about fungi, about the changing behavior of the fungi, the time for stands to flush back out with new needles, the drop in oxygen, the nitrogen never absorbed, the next potential change coming, what lies ahead for all treelines. Within 100 miles of the. A dream of total measurement: to capture every dimension of one defoliation event: a dream confusing past into future. Holy to count every ring, within every fallen tree. To stop time from taking them.

People upset at being out of work. The partitioning of the forest. Strained, watch the tops of sugar maples for crown dieback. Watch skies for acid rain. People experimenting with rage. A streak of saffron, floating on down the road.

Early morning in the fields, midmorning in the fields, one ducks her head in the passenger seat of a truck. On a hill behind, another hides habitually, her family trained for a hundred years. Eugenics projects of the early twentieth century: well funded, mostly from private sources. Then a passage of laws. From investigation, to incarceration, to sterilization. Who's so rural now. Charting the course of *Human Betterment*! A muttering noise, its errors. Head for the hills, disconnection for survival. The weight given every such thing. A figure rests under the blanket of a French surname, under the need to eject a past from the self.

He was really looking for someone else.

A possum slows between fractured habitats.

Purges rolling down. Death, you don't believe / ? / —that ambience.

It's in bad taste.

Harbingers. Connected farmhouses grip some love.

The children remember the circus, circling under an oak tree.

Out of sight one solitary figure pauses on a porch overlooking hills, highest porch of the hills, highest of all the hills. Figure has always looked for a home on a hill, began in one house on a hill to the south, ended in another house on a hill in the north, sees both east and west from the house, east and west mark the nature of time. Figure descends to mark the lines of history on patches of land nearby. Figure ascends to write them down. See him moving past now? The dirt road leading to this house on this hill will always need to be reconstructed in the summer, and plowed frequently in the winter, and sometimes sanded for ice.

Reconcile yes and no, the happening in pain.

When did the first person . . . ?

Working the world: compressor forces images out, one at a time.

Bang.

Developer said, it wasn't worth it.

That flare: a birth, or an advent, or just an increment.

The children fuss to be carried.

One ankle lifting its pinch toward the textured ceiling, dropping back to the floor. Inside bump thoughts of disconnection, and sometime later a darkening valley. Geological projections: Where is its cut, its sense of shear, the end of land? Or: Who is your medical advocate, etcetera, and when do you really need one. Moving this weight around inside the mind. Insects hover delicately, under the last stripe of sun; huddled mint, under the last sun; a scent loosed by the stand of pines, under the last sun. Remember when you could walk at noon, casting the least shadow. Take a few symbolic steps.

Secrets: the children play behind a closed door.

Blue heron holds in place, its place is in a pond, the pond's place is to the north of the road, water rises, water sinks. Now the heron boats back and forth alone above electrical lines. You are silver and gold. Tail feathers ellipse away. The heron's nest is not alone. Its colony arcs trees and bushes, the ones down by the river. Pick one:

- *Photography is an emotional response to light*
- *Rules are, by definition, simple—and animals are not*
- [X]

Drones, the neighbor above likes the view, someone else's machine flies over the forest, over a small hawk in the tree, over the parcel set aside with a conservation lien. Neighbor with infinite horizons surveils the future, its debts blanketed. The innumerable debts of others. Out of sight below, the laundry thumps, laundry dependent on water from a low-yield well, cold laundry today, warm laundry tomorrow, a daily tithe until the well will finally run dry. High above the curve of the earth, we bend our longing.

That other we, experimenting with boundaries, jockeying at the car in front, actual speeds meaningless. Acting out angry intervals fuck off squeak my bumper. A passage divided into intervals, the rate of potential connections. What is the nature of our shared passage of fucking-off bumpers and forgetting-squeaks? Rituals of attack, breaching routine distances among forms. The ones who never go too far. The ones who do. Erasure of the car, the scene, and the road.

The children leave pieces from trucks outside, forgotten.

A spiral staircase wraps around a dead trunk, bicycle wheels string together to make a goat fence, also some large earthenware jars, half a car's exterior.

Stationary things, observing a curve.

Bang.

The fluttering light slows. It holds the breath, so pain can rise.

What the dead laid there before us.

The spike of standing up.

Doctor's orders. All in shades of blue.

Motors, a lot delineated by the edge of one motor sound and the start of the next, the ingenuities, the deafness, the triumphalism of noise, the way the noise of its triumph carries across valleys, windows of time separating one motorized sound from the next. You are silver and gold, *I am lucid*. If not, truth is motor noise. The world floods with motor photos, with odors of gas and batteries. Stop your mind, hold blanks in the story, bob elimination through the memory.

One child will have a scar along an eye.

A lime-green conflict. The bicyclist zags side to side across the damp road. There the road runs straight, the cyclist does not, a progression inexplicable and slow. Hang back. Continue forward. An identity unspools. What comes together or togethers without. Online maps show a gun company on the road: there. Newer neighbors see only blank. Turn away to the ridge over there, a piedmont runs down the other side, its rhythms given other names. What is it that seems? Guns you had in mind. The face of one possible future, meeting you on the way down. Death keeps that one to herself.

The children on the hill shout, grayed out.

On the outbound path, figure intersecting with a child who carries an armful of flowers down the road. Yellow sunflowers, zinnias, orange, magenta. Both walk on the moving shadows of leaves, walk among them. The black flies riding humid waves toward orifices in the face, black flies that should already be gone. On the inbound path, intersecting with a town machine, its mowing arm reaching down to its right: eliminating lilies, jewelweed, Queen Anne's lace, milkweed, tall grasses, joe-pye weed, unbloomed asters, unopened cocoons, living strips of orange white pink green roadside. *The border lining one love is another one.*

IN THE BACK OF THE MIND

Figure reaching for beets sees time in the rinds of squash. Consume this increment now, initiate the next: maintain lines of action. That striped squash lasts until midwinter, the blue one until nearly spring. Shimmers of chicken wire once compressed by a bear. This figure pulling on garlic scans for fat cloves, plans for fatter cloves, sees the slim for the current year, sees two leaves, three slim leaves turning yellow, hands on the clock clicking together, alarm going off. The now-and-future fear of time seizing with soured seeds, diminished bees. Form inclines over azure borage flowers, the now, their white centers winking in a cup of red wine. A cup-sized firmament. Far below, the bedrock.

The children call out for good dreams.

Incendiary women of other times, your restlessness smolders. Angry fathers write retro books claiming ownership of the hills, their backs turned to the highest ridgelines. Pairings and partnerships, cutouts. You are silver and gold and lucid. Incendiary women, *your numerous presence*. Your shift appears fantastic gold to the father only if isolated and artisanal in one *atmosphere of virtue*. Would-be patriarchs measure words from your numerous undifferentiated: the noncompliant mass with their *barren view*. Don't you know the sixties were supposed to be for fun? Not your fun, another kind. Figures witness to the limit around a love. Stop your mind. Which one should come to meet you?

The children want flashlights.

A second striding shape affirms the empty space where beavers recently were. Shrubs expanding across the pond since the storm, shading into edges of autumn. Lodge covered in ever-larger living plants, still distinct from the scene around it. Pond, marsh, meadow. Successions to come depend on the absence or presence of beavers. What fills the space inside that too-green mound? Neighbor looks off toward the ridge. Did you ever figure it out, which one to love?

Low-flying aircraft, here are we, under the jetpath of descendent furies.

Praise, we have accepted ourselves.

The foundations of our homes tremble through trajectories.

All sharp triangles, the squadron returns to its base.

Then we met out there on the road.

The children huddle in blankets.

Power snapped out. Dreaming the sorrows of electricians. The silver and bronze network, woven cooperatives. This service territory, in its nameless contorted geometry. Engage. Power snaps on. Power snaps off. Is this the new . . . Power locks on. Longing they stopped at dawn. The green comes on in waves.

A horse passed through. The smell of horse hovers above the asters, above the bee balm, above the dirt. Dusty waves, where the form of the horse recently displaced that air. Later no horse will come. Do you remember the smell of absent horse?

THIRD

Bus driver keeps time, time winds through foothills. Bus stops here, stops there, when the bus stops everything else is supposed to halt, everything except the children running every which way, most of them every which way, dropping sticks into a stream is more important than a bus. Every once in a while, a child's gaze stops back at the yellow bus. Schedule change. Which dreams of childhood, and where will you project them? Bus driver keeps time, time watches a crumpled leaf float down the water inside the ditch. It's time to go.

Something in the ceaseless chatter of migrating geese. Would be, would be. Disturbances within the landscape. One figure remembers: barbed wire embedded in the bark. It's a clue: barbs once divided cows. At the bend of every hill, the scratched lens and a would-be truth.

Chainsaws sounding across an early fall.

Since nations remain contained within borders, they are forced to witness themselves as none other than conflict, as the source most valued. Who was I to exist.

At odds, our allotments. Then the replication, those empty architectures wherever resistance folds. Parking lots, driveways, the signatures in heat. Easements toward futures more conformable to fears. Absent of public toilets.

Transform your face, that's nice. That is so creemee. A blue sky so dark it turned . . .

Tourist holds up a paper then lets it drop, looks, squints, looks again, lifts a device and lets it drop. Tourists here and tourists there, some want to get lost, others fear getting lost. Inside the outside. Figures holding up one economy while irrelevant to another. These publics, facing down. Looking from outside toward an inside, or outside toward an outside; wondering where the inside went or some other thing entirely. Wait. Where did that Olympian go?

The general public requires toilets. There is no toilet. To be for the general public, [X] must have a public toilet. The public toilet: key to the public kingdom: the hollow of civic need. Portables, their compliant refuge, contents routinely removed, dumped across fields overlooking the river. Fields occasionally flooding into the river. The lake itself. The uniformed figure nods and nods, whether you thought you were public or not, see, the water.

Watchful, a figure assessing all likelihoods of winter. Autumnal equinox hovering nearby. Scratches from the rescue dog, still aggressive, lines up and down the driver-side door. The mint patch: its lines expanded toward the flowers. A wood, one bee. Monstrosities of the civic sort. Keep them to yourself as you vanish into the road. *Polis was to be and to be so hit*. Same work, less money. Return this contract within 48 hours. What is this *underemployed* anyway, and we called it history.

The children rescue a grasshopper.

On the working side of the mountain. Wind power facility an attractive energy bounded turbine-sited infrasound without *undue adverse impacts* on the mountain attractiveness. Assessment, mobile perspectives from certain more distant roads. Posterior assessment, wind keens and hushes through the foundations of public good siding a ridgeline. In your sights. What does a ridgeline mark?

The children dig in the dirt at their finding place.

Once upon a time [X] had a great mill. Fingertip short by a measure, shortened by a measure, a measure of movement from the machine, or a false start from the finger. Woodworking, a now-scene of fabrication: the saw in the hands of inattentive, of young, the saw sniping bits of ill-directed plank across the room. Realignments. Once upon a time this village was bigger than all the rest, even the city on the lake. Now its desperate ranks will expand. An elder holds up what remains of the finger. Its majority, and a puff of evaporating time.

Light rests gently on the hard-packed road, hovers on the frames from leaves. Lengths of clay and gravel disappear with the passing of your feet. When the oil truck came, its people were rotating in generation, the younger in hands-on present, the elder talking history through shadows in the garage. Eyes wrinkling around the passage from one family service to the next, within a morning. The passage between one commercial service and the next, within a season. The old and new rubber boots needed for the job, set out under a looping light.

One child whimpers: words that will bring bad dreams.

WITHIN ONE
REMOVE

Unexpectedly stark: shadows against the road. The first yellow leaves advance down it, their noise trailing in the same direction as the latest car. Alter your face, turn it toward some other, is there any other face for firmament. Let dark consume the symbols, a self you no longer need.

The children draw outrageous animals.

Smoke, a dissipated smoke, a not-yet smoke, those first yellowed leaves going past. Figure of the neighbor regarding the burn pile. Size of the pickup truck pointed in its direction. Methodical wait, each discrete wait one step toward. The many moments of the outdoor. Winter still at one remove, yet its looping light, facets platooning in the mind. Silver and gold from passing headlights, the closing of these hours.

Grader of roads throws a machine into gear. A course charted. Ridgeline in the back of the mind, is that dissonance? Warning: low shoulder. The body, the body claims a damaged shoulder, warning urgently of rain. The ridgeline behind a stand of aspens. Grader proceeds, the ridgeline moves into a line of sight. Can't look up to grasp its appearance. Not now, when only the ache means anything. First there was blue. Then came gray. Elsewhere, yet not so far and to the east: a place called the piedmont, inside some other time.

The children build a creature of buckets. It looks downhill.

Cacophonies.

Who *take for clarity the jaundiced laughter of shadows*, flexing.

People accelerating through mind and rain, inside silver, ballooning outside the unwelcome, commands commanding who cares.

A neighbor returned home. With assistance from hospice.

Why fog strains toward the sky.

Dissonance,

its endless ridgelines.

A roadside progresses in the colors of its detritus. One length of old needles fallen, an ordinary autumn drop, now gone orange. One length of leaves fallen, already adding up to brown. A resistant chicory plant standing, its two bright-blue flowers, the only flowers surviving this segment. Less than 100 miles from the. One length of curved twigs and branches, and if a snake died now, it would blend right in. Beaver marsh accompanying several segments with tall grass, shrubs, cattails, open water. Then back: to the branches, to the leaves, to the needles. How lucid? All that is solid melts into sediment.

Left hand, right hand, the children try, hesitantly.

The neighbor left off burning piles.

The wail of a fishercat in the night cuts through one house. Two houses.

Pain happens this day kept close. Market the pain? Be creemee!

The child whose father was flying the fighter jet.

A liquid intersect. Cupped in hills, a merging of disparate things.

The children turn storage boxes out onto the floor.

Skipping: a military craft maneuvers far above, scraping out bits of sky.

Blink at the sharpness of the autumn sun, back for an early afternoon, its skips. To walk along a dirt road in hills equals to pass from one color into another color.

Also from one frequency into another frequency. A chain of motors pierces the mind. Those who disappeared. Say it, don't say it, try to reroute the weight of the senses, their orientation, their power, make it good, say nothing about the line. Remember dust from a horse. Animals we they you me. Fabricate a moving silence.

This way some realtor has passed, marking the nearest house for sale.

FOURTH

This time there will be no construction on the floodplain, in the center of town, otherwise short on water. Are you there? A social death, flickering. Maybe next time. Dignity inside a shroud, under the rough language of disbelief, deep inside our personal vaults, the release of each expanse, then another behind it. Things I, a personal connectivity agent, cannot connect, fuck-and-all joining in the breeze. Nonplus. To cage I cage you cage he cages she cages it cages they cage you-plural cage we cage keeping cages to ourselves. Are we still on the ground? A thousand deported mothers, would you meet them in their grief. Unyoke: suppression of *thing* below the plane of sight. A firework winding spirals inside a vault. A wheel in the striking train of a clock. Retake your timeless course. It is the slated hour, and someone just walked in.

Snow falls toward snow falls toward snow falls toward close snow falls toward snow falls toward looping snow falls toward snow falls toward skip snow falls I forget toward snow falls toward

OUR

NEE

Blown snow. Sideways, seen snow on the forest's pillows, its cradles and mounds. Shelter from an old blowdown. White in waves. No sign of your own face, your borrowed hours. Or to whom the slant snow speaks. Flames taut in a burning stove. Keep [X]. That one's for your self.

Ice, and the condition of teeth, among hills. Grief for a grasped-at gone. At whose base twinkled lights. Erasures. *When it appeared around the bend, throwing out snow in sheets, like spray from a motorboat.* Someone tries to answer. Back to the night's disarticulations. Silences, these become laws not gone but closing, or astray on slick data. Law: the craft of forming receptacles, in which to cup our force.

The children point sleds at a grove of trees.

Get out and walk, fine. Walking on ice, casting self outward. A walk-on part in the dream: that crossing, a tendency to emanate. An overly familiar question. Then the figures flipped into screens, into death's biometric embrace. Did you trace the course of your personal migration. Skip: to outlines of humans, centuries past, leaning against the land: all along, their shadows followed the edges of the ice. A child whose brother was flying the fighter jet, deported fathers. Me you us they. Skip: slipped, and fell, flat on its sheet. *The swooping maneuver allows jets to complete their landing efficiently to open the runway back up for civilian and commercial aircraft traffic.*

The children demand help. They give confusing instructions.

On the eastern end of the road: Huntington. Valleyed memories with upland desires manifest downhill at the 1870 town church, with belltower, converted into a library, near the river. Holding what forms were, what they are, what may become.

[What is it that seems so, and who is not? Sightings in cavernous shadow: as the crow, shadows from high church ceilings, beached canoe, imaging all of the earth, cuddles, life-size stuffie predators fairies fairy houses mushrooms, overdue dragons gargoyles leprechauns African gods indigenous creation, astronomy additional fairies origin mysteries, Norse gods, organic gardening, signs and voices inside these walls, skating edges strokes carve, attempts at Green Mountain principles, Danish design, the more polite aspects of the underground railroad, order, polar bears all about soccer, ponds, closed ecstatics, envision Gaia's garden, riding up and riding down: did any of it grow heavy with life.]

[Voices, view from outside the earth, signs, when first ski hills went up, tension, those signs and voices, griffins gnomes wands interplanetary travel donations, murder team journalists, voices inside, these walls, these orders, these experiences, back then when so many moved in, what they used to call death, of dust from stars, audiences, and sales, ritual golem Holmes and red, who could afford to go, tension, inside these walls disorder, who will pay to put it out that's how to put out fires, chimneys and how to build a better, disordered signs and voices sexed astronomical constellations minus astrological constellations equals one, signs, orderly, mythological heroine all the echo magnetism prison scandal quit, the electrician said it was so, what stalks down that shadowed road, the snow from stars, their gravel, voices inside these walls: here we are, they say, right here.]

[More and more they turn out despite the ice, donations sent from abroad passed over from houses uphill, scratched dented creased fragments of our time, we are saffron dropped from stars, archeological finds druids detectives ski bums fences shrubbery, tales and signs, travel here travel there hello here up inside hills hello there, voices. Riding up the rope tow, then beyond, up at the ridgeline, blown sideways, stripped bare of all data. Sightings: the crows hop. Held inside, or loosed all throughout the mind?]

A skunk made itself known in the night. Its pawprints too. Again the slush, top-down, passed off as the face of the partitioned people, generally speaking, squeaking, it skips, another face obscured in the space between. Resembling your dignity. *Thy stately rhetorick, is such a non sequitur.* Silver dust dropped from stars or horses. Sequence, no, a no sequence. When a you, as a form, has to start in and out of a deep. A non, the dark, in non sequitur. Or the motionless light of some day. Out of its stillness, say, everything else was walking.

The children, a birthday.

Deer who toed the tracks I made, knee-deep, across snow.

The crisscross of our need. Am I sick yet? Those disappearing faces,
their dusty multitudes.

Keep going, they said, *just keep going.*

Acer saccharum. Treetops draw away. We draw away. Early sap runs clear. The sun's
lucidity in the sap.

Things that blow through cracks in the mind.

If you're going to do it, it had best be now.

Ambient music but of which kind?

- *Shines light in all directions from directly above the image—like a light bulb.*
- *Shines light across an entire plane—like the sun.*
- *Casts an elliptical beam of light.*

Figure in the sugarhouse. Where once were birthed lambs, now are birthed treelines, sprung back into the sheep-nibbled sky. Figure mounts lines, pegs one tree to the next, seeks out the slight declination. You are silver and bronze and properly weighted. This one installs the first sights of some plastic web, funneling sap across the land. Years ago a moose walked into a line and dragged it miles off into the forest. Here and now some cicatrix shows, a barb under the tree's grown bark. Some cicatrix under the figure's thick clothes. The now-and-future fear of the roots slowing time, the diminished trees.

When no one else is looking, the children dance, like astronauts dance.

Stretching liquid into lines: A body secret even unto itself, branching. How expansive its opacity, the opening rip, its ability to glare, the glare of enforcement dragging future walls behind. Ground crumbling, and surreptitious words insist, the people already consented. No the people did not. Who are these people again? A remake, a world in vision, it skips on a generality. I live in generalities. No I do not. Each silver valley a vault, under its own dome of sky. Shagbarked hickories embrace baby bats. Did you forget your hemispheres. The northern forest, *see it before it changes.* A snap: from a tree, or the dome, or the earth.

As meltwater runs, so runs sap. Speculate about the lifetime of a tree, its future years, the likelihood of drought. Speculate about the duration of the well reaching farther below. Unseen folded layers keeping their crazy pitch. Divine with your rod where water pools, drill for a well wherever. Hit fractures, hit bedding, hit foliation planes, tap recharging waters. These your downward lines. Envision bedrock from one plate or another, with and without elevated radionuclides in its veins, and foothills in spaces between. Measure a water level for the first well. Measure here-time into dreaming, suspect an aquifer, sniff for the immense grandeur of that aquifer, one to outlast them all, rural foothill gold. Measure the money not saved up to pay for drilling wells. Hydrogeology speaks: it can't read the lifetime of any well, not within asymmetries raised in the hill. Put a well down and wait. This is what leads to a fear of time. This is also what protects you.

All that is solid slumps into mud. Only in the illusion of freedom does existence. Gritty images, hard to read, obscure: clear as mud. For mud is clear, mud is timely, mud reliable. Its organisms respire. Mud undoes form, remakes form, mud carries infinite starry worlds. Does mud need lines to merge? Viscous slurry takes its own shapes. Still waiting for some future role. But mud, it comes when you call. Mud slaps life-forms all over your boots, all over the car, into the wheel wells of every last pickup.

When no one else is listening, the children sing.

Road reflects in the eyes. Treading one soft wet side. How the vernal equinox presents but eludes the eye. Another isolate figure at the bend. Let's consider loneliness in the eyes holding road, and also mud from bats and foxes. For just one moment the sun's center passes a line, balancing the day against night. In the north, spring, all forms tilting toward sun. A new astronomical year. Disengage meets reengage, some methods for survival. Grasp your new axis. The everyday tips under our feet. By evening. We will see that it was already tipping. Me you us they, left to catch up to splitting ground. Who held power inside their hands? Try to gain perspective, what you get instead is glinting. It's the altered angle of sun against this gravel, or it's those distant figures.

ACKNOWLEDGMENTS

Excerpts from this book, sometimes in different versions, were first published in English or translation by the following journals:

Acrobata (in Portuguese translation by Floriano Martins): "Chainsaws sounding . . ."; "Light rests gently . . ."; "Once upon a time . . ."; "On the working side of the mountain . . ."; "Watchful . . ."

Almost Island: "Ice, and the condition of teeth . . ."; "A roadside progresses . . ."; "Skipping: a military . . ."; "This time there will be no construction . . ."

Clade Song: "A skunk . . ."; "Is there an us . . ."

Distropika (with Spanish translations by Tina Escaja): "Cacophonies . . ."; "Grader of roads . . ."; "A neighbor returned . . ." (as "A neighbor's return . . ."); "A roadside progresses . . ."

El Nieuwe Acá (with Spanish translations by Tina Escaja): "Builder of one's own home . . ."; "Figure at a screen . . ."; "Isolated figure trots . . ."

The Hopper: "Where the north lies . . ."

Lana Turner: A Journal of Poetry and Opinion: "Chainsaws sounding . . ."; "The general public requires . . ."; "Light rests gently . . ."; "Once upon a time . . ."; "On the outbound path . . ."; "On the working side of the mountain . . ."; "Smoke . . ."; "*Something in the ceaseless chatter* . . ."; "Unexpectedly stark . . ."; "Watchful . . ."

Seedings: "Blue heron . . ."; "Figure in the sugarhouse . . ."; "Motors, a lot . . ."; "Tourist holds up a paper . . ."

I appreciate the recognition of earlier versions of the manuscript in competitions run by Omnidawn and *The Hopper*.

I'm grateful to writers, editors, and translators for the conversations and remarks that helped me bring this collection together across years, among them Cal Bedient, Roberto Tejada, Reina María Rodríguez, Forrest Gander, Daniel Borzutzky, Urayoán Noel, Marcelo Morales, Tina Escaja, and om ulloa.

Special thanks to Srikanth Reddy, Katie Peterson, Douglas Kearney, and Rosa Alcalá for selecting this book for the Phoenix Poets series and for offering illuminating comments that shaped the end of this process. I would like to thank David Olsen, associate editor at the University of Chicago Press, for his work with me. I am also very grateful to McKenna Smith for extended, patient attention during the copyediting phase to the unconventional uses of language in this work. I would also like to offer my thanks to Mint Liu for the design of this work.

Love and Gratitude

To my husband, Brian, and my children for their unconditional support of this writing and for contributing so many things out of which this book is made—above all their constant, playful curiosity about a hill, a road, two towns, and their small libraries. Special thanks to Brian for coediting the images with me.

To my childhood friend and reading buddy, Abby Smith, for being such a firm supporter of this project.

To my parents for introducing me to ever-expanding realms of music, operating through dissonance and harmony.

NOTES

Preface

IX.　Origin: Formed within English, by compounding: Oxford English Dictionary, s.v. "foot-hill (n.)," last modified July 2023, https://doi.org/10.1093/OED/5304787419.

FIRST

7.　*Over the lake a white wall was advancing, driving foam before it. The mountains sank down in the white, the wind began to sing*: Elliott Merrick, *From This Hill Look Down* (Brattleboro, VT: Stephen Daye Press, 1934), 92.

7.　*The rain is rain, and for me and my lips and body*: Elliott Merrick, *From This Hill Look Down*, 94.

9.　*who grows blunt through premonitions*: René Char, "Argument," in *Furor and Mystery, and Other Writings*, trans. Mary Ann Caws and Nancy Kline (Boston: Black Widow Press, 2010), 39.

13.　within 100 miles of an external border: "The Constitution in the 100-Mile Border Zone," American Civil Liberties Union, August 21, 2014, https://www.aclu.org/documents/constitution-100-mile-border-zone.

13.　*bipolar clash*: Heather Nicol, *The Fence and the Bridge: Geopolitics and Identity along the Canada-US Border* (Ontario, Canada: Wilfrid Laurier University Press, 2015), 199.

13.　*The center operates 24 hours a day, seven days a week, 365 days a year*: "Law Enforcement Support Center," U.S. Immigration and Customs Enforcement, accessed August 15, 2020, https://www.ice.gov/lesc. This language was taken from the official website of U.S. Immigration and Customs Enforcement (ICE), the largest investigative agency within the nation's Department of Homeland Security. It described the Law Enforcement Support Center located in Williston, Vermont.

SECOND

25. *Human Betterment*: Nancy L. Gallagher, *Breeding Better Vermonters: The Eugenics Project in the Green Mountain State* (Hanover, NH: University Press of New England, 1999). This phrase is from the title of Vermont's 1931 sterilization law, reprinted as an appendix in *Breeding Better Vermonters*.

30. *Photography is an emotional response to light*: This is from a quotation posted to social media by photographer Jaime Permuth.

30. *Rules are, by definition, simple—and animals are not*: Bernd Heinrich, *The Geese of Beaver Bog* (New York: Harper Collins, 2004), xiv.

33. COME TO MEET YOU: Paul Celan, *Microliths: Posthumous Prose*, trans. Pierre Joris (New York: Contra Mundum Press, 2020), 57. This phrase is from the longer passage "Yourself: someone walking, nothing more. Wiped out, your memory, done with what had been, given up, what had been known. You walk along, and this one here should come to meet you."

37. *The border lining one love is another one*: Marcelo Morales, *The Star-Spangled Brand*, trans. Kristin Dykstra (Houston: Veliz Books, 2025). The core images originate from a line from prose poetry. Morales wrote, "El límite del amor es otro amor." This statement slowly shifts in transit across languages. Another rendition that appears in this book is "The edge defining one desire interrupts the forward motion of another."

40. *your numerous presence*: René Char, "Refusal Song," in *Furor and Mystery, and Other Writings*, 81.

40. *atmosphere of virtue*: David Mamet, *South of the Northeast Kingdom* (Washington, D.C.: National Geographic, 2002),77. This quote is the first of two from Mamet's book, in which he seeks to define a "regional mind" operative in Vermont.

40. *barren view*: David Mamet, *South of the Northeast Kingdom*, 29. This quote is from Mamet's version of a "regional mind."

42. *Praise, we have accepted ourselves*: René Char, "A Youth," in *Furor and Mystery, and Other Writings*, 47.

THIRD

46. *Something in the ceaseless chatter of migrating geese*: Heinrich, *The Geese of Beaver Bog*, xi.

50. *Polis was to be and to be so hit*: Nathaniel Mackey, "As If It Were 'This Is Our Music,'" *Poetry*, June 2014, https://www.poetryfoundation.org/poetrymagazine/poems/57018/as-if-it-were-this-is-our-music.

51. *undue adverse impacts*: Jody M. Prescott, "Ridgelines and the National Security Implications of Commercial Wind Energy Development in Vermont," *Vermont Journal of Environmental Law* 13, no. 4: 673.

51. public good: A phrase used in legal claims and determinations regarding land usage.

58. *take for clarity the jaundiced laughter of shadows*: René Char, "Mirage of the Peaks," in *Furor and Mystery, and Other Writings*, 431.

FOURTH

67. *When it appeared around the bend, throwing out snow in sheets, like spray from a motorboat*: Elliott Merrick, *From This Hill Look Down*, 171.

68. *The swooping maneuver allows jets to complete their landing efficiently to open the runway back up for civilian and commercial aircraft traffic*: "Learn More About F-35 Operations of the Vermont Air National Guard," Vermont National Guard, F-35 Program, accessed February 26, 2023, https://vt.public.ng.mil/About/Our-Missions/F-35-Program/.

70. *Thy stately rhetorick, is such a non sequitur*: Philotimus, *The warre betwixt nature and fortune*, comp. Brian Melbancke (London, 1583).

72. *Shines light in all directions from directly above the image—like a light bulb*: "Add Lighting Effects," Photoshop User Guide, Adobe, https://helpx.adobe.com/photoshop/using/add-lighting-effects1.html.

72. *Shines light across an entire plane—like the sun*: "Add Lighting Effects," Photoshop User Guide, Adobe, https://helpx.adobe.com/photoshop/using/add-lighting-effects1.html.

72. *Casts an elliptical beam of light*: "Add Lighting Effects," Photoshop User Guide, Adobe, https://helpx.adobe.com/photoshop/using/add-lighting-effects1.html.

74. *see it before it changes*: A common phrase, explicitly applied to Cuba, from news coverage of tourism in the 21st century. It is not spoken but implied in relation to the northern forests.